HOOKS, L

Other titles in the series

Baits
Rods and Reels
Float and Leger Rigs

HOOKS, LINES AND KNOTS
for coarse fishing

By Ken Whitehead
Illustrated by Russell Birkett

WARD LOCK

© Text and illustrations Ward Lock Limited 1989

First published in Great Britain in 1989
by Ward Lock Limited, 8 Clifford Street
London W1X 1RB

Designed by Bob Vickers
Text filmset in Times
by Litho Link Ltd, Welshpool, Powys

Printed and bound in Great Britain

British Library Cataloguing in Publication Data
Whitehead, Ken, *1930 Aug. 10* —
  Hooks, lines and knots for coarse fishing. —
  (Fishing skills pocket book).
  1. Coarse fish. Angling
  I. Title II. Series
  799.1'1

  ISBN 0-7063-6825-8

CONTENTS

PREFACE

That fascinating young scallywag Huckleberry Finn used string and a bent pin when he went trying for catfish. But while a feeding fish is not aware of the difference between the pin and a modern machine-made hook, Huck's chances of landing better and bigger fish would have been very much improved. Prehistoric man used the materials at hand to make hooks out of bone and even flint and hunted fish with them.

Ken Whitehead tells the interesting story of the modern hook and describes, accompanied by Russell Birkett's excellent black-and-white drawings, the salient parts of the hook, what the angler should look for and how he can test its quality.

Above the hook, part of the terminal tackle, the line carries floats, weights and swivels and then leads through the rod rings to the reel. Some of these items need knots for attachment but when tied in today's universal nylon monofilament knots can spell danger, for nylon is notorious in that knots slip easily.

The author explains the properties of this man-made miracle we call nylon and then runs through those knots used most often by anglers and known to hold under stress.

Until recently, lead split shot was the universal method of weighting floats to ensure that they were sensitive and correctly balanced. But then it was claimed, some say unjustly, that discarded lead shot was responsible for poisoning swans. Now, legislation is in force banning the use of lead for angling use below a certain weight, therefore all references to split shot and shotting patterns in this book and the others in the series refer to the various commercially produced lead substitutes.

The author of this series, Ken Whitehead, is an all-round fisherman happy with whatever species is found in the water he happens to be fishing. His biggest fish is a pike well in excess of 30 lb and he can include carp in the early 20s among the many entries in his fishing diary. He has come to feel that while the pike's lifestyle includes the taking of live fish, the use of livebaiting is not for him.

He has written or co-authored over 20 books covering every aspect of the sport and was one of the innovators of the pictorial approach to teaching new and would-be anglers the tricks of the trade.

Ken Whitehead is as keen on shooting and the countryside in general as he is on fishing and contributes to several magazines. His first shooting book is due to be published this year.

The artist responsible for the clear, no-nonsense black-and-white drawings is 23-year-old Russell Birket a young graduate with a BA(Hons) degree in Graphic Information and Design from Falmouth. The illustrations in this series are his first major contribution to the field of book illustration and he intends to pursue a career in publishing.

Len Cacutt, general editor of the series, has been closely concerned with angling publishing in all its forms, having himself written a number of books and compiled and edited angling books, magazines and encyclopedias for the leading publishers, and was Founder Editor of an angling newspaper.

INTRODUCTION

It is obvious that fish will be able to see everything that is below the surface, assuming of course that the water is clear and not thick with suspended matter. In fact, fish can also see through the surface film although here their vision is to some extent distorted. These facts indicate that great care should be exercised by the angler at all times, especially when it comes to the selection and presentation of his terminal tackle. The items of which it is composed may cost little when compared with the price of a new rod or reel. They are called terminal tackle because they are literally at the end of the line — and the angler really has to know just what he should, and should not do if he is going to hook his fish. In this section of the book there are three items that we must consider in connection with the angler's terminal tackle; hooks, line, and knots — which are the means of joining the two together.

HOOKS

HOOKS: INTRODUCTION

Without doubt, hooks are the most important item in the angler's tackle box. This basic element of the angler's tackle dates back thousands of years to the Stone Age. Hooks made from flint and bone are known from those times and they have barbs and points very similar to today's machine-made ones (1).

1

4000 year old
hook from late
Stone Age
made of bone

Modern hook

Unless the hook is reliable there is a possibility
that the fish will either fail to be hooked, or it
will break free. There is a bewildering display
of hooks on the market and many of them are
described later in this book, but at first the
angler should concentrate on a few of the
standard models available, leaving the
purchase of those that are for specialist
purposes until they are required.

For most of his time at the waterside the coarse
fisherman will be using single hooks tied to the
end of his line. There are also other kinds of
hooks available that are welded together either
as double or as treble hooks. These are usually
used on spinning lures and on plugs. (2)

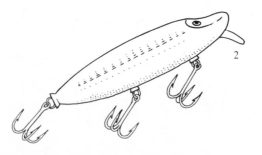

Occasionally hooks are mounted one above
the other as an aid to carrying a bait in such a
way that it can easily be seen by fish. The
Pennell tackle is one such method, where two
hooks are tied to the line one above the other

in what is described as tandem style. Another method, using three hooks, is called Stewart tackle. (3)

3

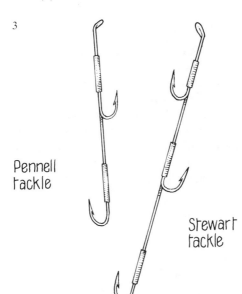

Pennell
tackle

Stewart
tackle

HOOK ANATOMY

The majority of fishing hooks are mass-
produced by machine from wire. It is
important that this wire must have a good
temper, which means that it should not bend
out of shape easily, and that it should be thin.
Testing the temper of a hook is best carried
out by holding it by the shank and pulling just
above the point with a pair of fine pliers. There
should be give, but no straightening. (4)

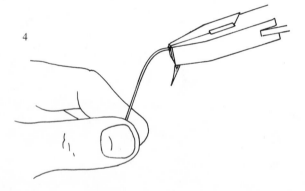

4

- The various parts of a hook have names,
  and it is better to understand the technical
  terms that are used — especially if you are
  trying to describe something in a tackle

shop. The diagram here describes the various parts. (5)

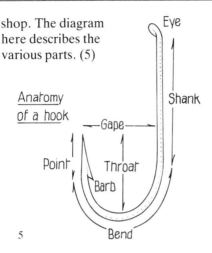

Anatomy of a hook

Eye

Shank

— Gape —

Point

Throat

Barb

Bend

5

■ Hooks that must have extra strength — those used for really powerful fish such as large pike and salmon — are not produced from wire, but are forged from heavy metal, which means they are not often used in general float fishing, but have applications when the angler is freelining a bait which is intended to be taken as it sinks, or lies on the bottom. Carp fishermen find these hooks useful. (6)

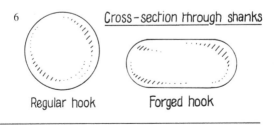

Cross-section through shanks

Regular hook   Forged hook

Bends

The bend of the hook (see Pic. 5) will affect the way that a bait is presented. It can also influence the direction in which the hook is lodged into the fish's mouth when the angler strikes.

- The Limerick bend has a sharp angle and is regarded by many as being difficult for a fish to release itself from. (7)

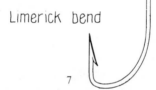

Limerick bend

7

- Much favoured by the coarse angler for worm fishing the round bend has a wide gape which connects easily with the mouth. (8)

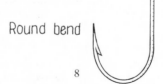

Round bend

8

■ A bend called the Viking (a manufacturer's trade name) is sharp-angled and turns back towards the shank (see Pic. 5). This helps prevent a fish from breaking free. (9)

Viking bend

9

■ Most popular in coarse fishing, the simple crystal bend is used universally, especially when maggot is the bait, either singly or in a bunch. (10)

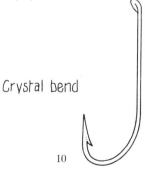

Crystal bend

10

■ The Model Perfect is a round bend with a
  slightly off-set point developed by the
  manufacturers Allcocks. It is a design from
  which many other hooks were developed.
  The bends of hooks are not only measured
  in relation to the gape — they are also
  measured in relation to the angle with the
  shank of the hook. (11)

11

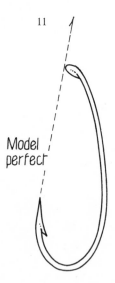

Model
perfect

■ The straight bend. Here the point runs in line with the shank of the hook. (12)

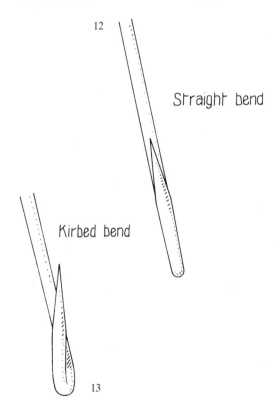

■ Kirbed bend — where the point is set to the right, out of line with the shank. This is favoured by many as being an aid in driving the hook home on the strike. (13)

Points

Making the entry into the mouth of the fish, a
point must be sharp, well shaped and fine. If
thick, clumsy and blunt it won't penetrate the
mouth area — especially in those species of
fish that have a large and well-developed bone
structure in the jaws, such as pike.

- Barbless points are favoured by the match
  angler where it is easy to unhook a fish,
  thus saving time. The angler must maintain
  a tight line all the time he is playing a fish
  on a barbless hook if it is not to be lost. (14)

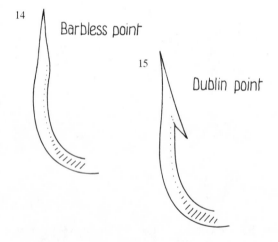

14 Barbless point

15 Dublin point

- Dublin points curve out, away from the
  shank of the hook. (15)

- Curved-in points have a curve towards the shank of the hook. (16)

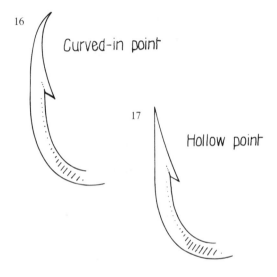

- Hollow point hooks have a straight outer edge. (17)

Barbs

The smallest part of a hook, yet the most important by far and one that frequently gives trouble. Always check the barb on every new hook that you use — there is often a dud one in a batch.

■ A barb deeply cut into the metal will
weaken the hook. (18)

■ Barbs set too far back from the point are
difficult to drive home — and can snap off
or break the line as the angler strikes. (19)

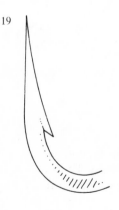

Eyes

On a hook, the means whereby a hook can be attached to the line. Always find the hook with the smallest eyes you can. The bigger the eye, the bigger the risk of the hook hanging sloppily at an angle to the line, or the line riding round the eye and weakening the nylon. Ideally, the line should just fit comfortably through the eye, neither too tight nor too loose.

- Tapered eyes. These are the most widely used eyes, and the curve should be complete, the end of the circle touching the shank of the hook so that line cannot slip free. (20)

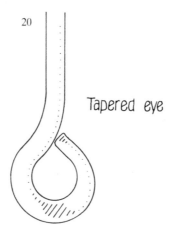

Tapered eye

- Ball eyes. These are similar to tapered eyes, but there is no taper in the diameter of the wire. Again, make sure that the ball is closed, or line may slip free. (21)

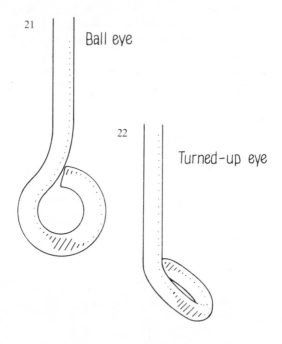

21 Ball eye

22 Turned-up eye

- Turned up eyes. The eye of the hook turns away from the point — an aid to hooking that some anglers insist on. Turned down eyes have the eye turning in towards the point, frequently found on hooks used for trout flies. (22)

- Double eyes. As the name suggests, these are found on double hooks — the eye turns away from the points. (23)

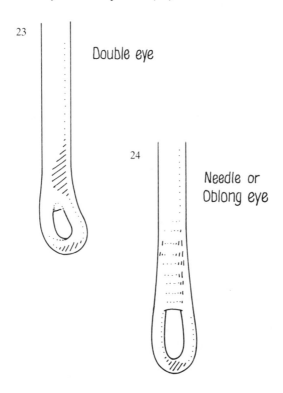

23 Double eye

24 Needle or Oblong eye

- Needle or oblong eyes are standard on treble hooks, allowing them to be whipped to traces or mounted to spoons or plugs. (24)

- Looped eyes are usually found on heavy hooks, especially in salmon fishing. The loop is turned up. (25)

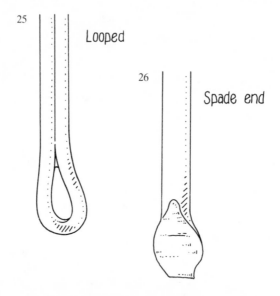

25 Looped

26 Spade end

- Spade-end hooks have flattened shanks instead of the usual eye, which allows the angler to tie his line direct onto the hook below the shank. In this position the line cannot slide free. The spade-end hook is widely used by coarse fishermen, especially the match angler, because the position of the knot on the shank ensures the point being driven upwards in a straight line. (26)

Shanks

The shank of the hook can affect the angle of penetration at its point. Generally the longer the shank is in relation to the eye, the smaller its angle of penetration must be. This means that the hook goes in easily but not very far. On the other hand the short shanked hook needs a more powerful strike to drive it home, but it will penetrate more deeply.

- The bait which is to be used should govern the length of shank. Cereals, worms, sweetcorn and similar baits need a hook with a long shank. Maggots should be used on a short-shanked hook. (27)

27

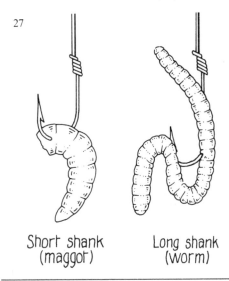

Short shank
(maggot)   Long shank
(worm)

■ Sliced shanks on hooks have a barb
designed to stop bait from slipping down
onto the bend and are often used in sea
fishing, but they also have a use for the
freshwater angler. Sliced shanks can be
purchased in small sizes. (28)

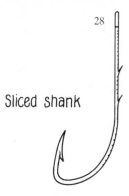

28

Sliced shank

Ready-Tied Hooks

Sold in packets, ready-tied hooks are attached
to a length of nylon which has a loop at the
other end so that it can be tied directly to the
reel line. The nylon is machine-whipped to the
hook, and not tied with a knot, the fine
whipping being varnished to prevent wear and
provide strength. As with most items of fishing
tackle, the more you pay, the better will be the
quality and hooks-to-nylon are no exception.
(29)

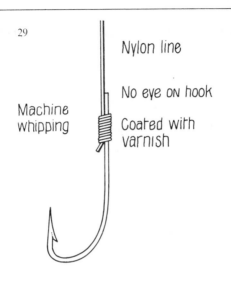

29

Nylon line

No eye on hook

Machine whipping

Coated with varnish

Multiple Hooks

Double and treble hooks are usually mounted on spinners and plugs, which are used for catching predatory fish including pike, perch, salmon and trout and so on. (30)

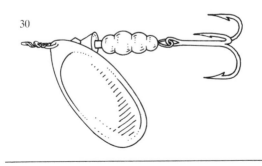

30

■ Salmon flies are frequently tied on double
hooks, the extra weight of two hooks
together helping the fly to sink in very fast
water. (31)

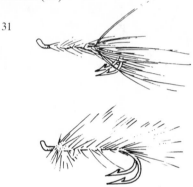

31

■ Treble hooks should be formed from fine
wire whenever small lures are being used.
Heavy, clumsy trebles can totally ruin the
spinning action of a delicate lure. (32)

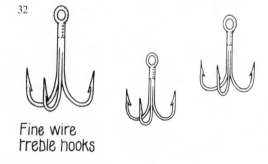

32

Fine wire
treble hooks

■ As with single hooks, trebles have sizes
  with the lower the number the larger the
  hook. A round bend is usual — there are
  alternatives, but rarely used. Look for a
  good, bronzed finish which will not rust.
  (33)

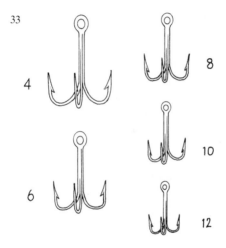

CHOOSING HOOKS

Only the best possible hook quality should be good enough, regardless of the price. When you are in the tackle shop buy your hooks by the box, but first ask to be allowed carefully to test several from it. Look for hooks that have a poor temper, have badly turned eyes, are too narrow in the gape, or have badly forged barbs (see Pic. 18, 19). Do not try to make one type of hook do the work of several — if you are worming use a long-shanked hook, then if you decide to change to maggots select a suitable, short-shanked hook. (34)

34   <u>Common hook faults</u>

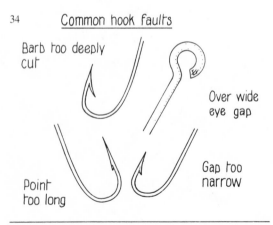

Barb too deeply cut

Over wide eye gap

Point too long

Gap too narrow

HOOK SIZES

As a general rule the size of the hook which will be selected is governed by the size of fish expected to be caught. The hook for a big 20 lb carp would hardly fit into the mouth of an 8 oz roach for instance. There are some exceptions to this rule, normally when small hooks have to be used for big fish. The tench is a good example — it has a relatively small and very soft mouth in comparison with its possible size and weight. (35)

35

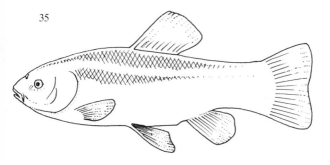

■ Hooks are sized in numbers, on an even scale from 2 to 30, and the lower the number the larger the hook will be. A size 2 hook is around ¾ in long, a size 20 about ⅛ of an

inch. Above size 2 the numbers have a suffix
/0, and run in consecutive numbers — 1/0,
2/0, 3/0 and so on. (36)

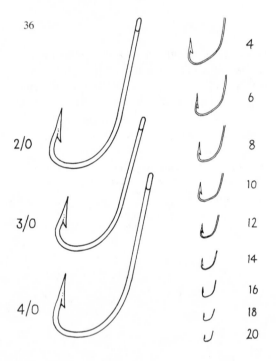

SHARPENING HOOKS

The best hook in the world will quickly blunt
in use. Just putting a bait on the hook can
cause it to lose its sharpness, and when the
hook is dragging the bottom it is suffering
constant wear. During and before fishing
hooks should be tested for sharpness against
the thumb-nail. (37)

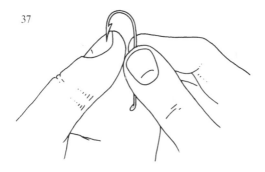

37

- To hone the point of a hook, use a
  sharpening stone purchased from the tackle
  shop. Make gentle strokes of the point along

the length of the stone and constantly check it as you do so. (38)

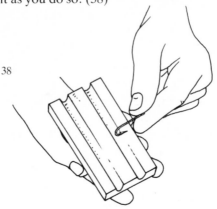

- The correct hook point is one that tapers gently, leaving a sharp-pointed, thin piece of metal for penetration. The wrong point has a short taper, leaving thick metal that will be difficult to drive home on the strike. (39)

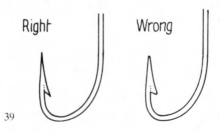

Right   Wrong

STORING HOOKS

Hooks left exposed to the damp will rust.
Hooks that are allowed to rattle around in
boxes of any sort will soon become blunt. Keep
your hooks folded in paper, stored in boxes. A
little thin oil will prevent them becoming rusty.
(40)

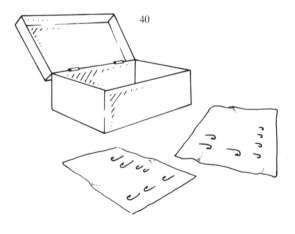

LINES AND KNOTS

LINES AND KNOTS: INTRODUCTION

Although nylon was discovered back in the 1930s it only became available to anglers after the end of the Second World War. At that time it was spooled in lengths of high breaking strain, and did not have the smoothness and suppleness which we expect in today's product. Monofilament today is manufactured by a process called double-extrusion. The basic material is forced through nozzles of varying diameter and as it emerges it hardens. Under a carefully adjusted tension, the nylon then passes through infra-red radiation and as it does so its diameter hardens and takes on the required breaking strain (see Pic. 43).

Present-day lines are very versatile and possess strength, fineness, and a certain degree of resistance to kinking. But all monofilament tends to stretch when placed under strain. This of course is very much to the angler's advantage during a hard strike or when a fish makes a sudden sharp pull.

Unfortunately, there is a tendency for a degree of this stretch to remain in the line afterwards — and it is something that can continue to build up, weakening until eventually there is a considerable reduction in line circumference and its subsequent strength.

Yet another characteristic of monofilament is the fact that nylon has the ability to absorb between 3 and 13 per cent of its own weight of water. By this means the breaking strain of the line can be reduced by as much as 10 per cent.

Although nylon deteriorates slowly it must be remembered that long exposure to light can weaken it, especially in diameters of low breaking strains. So when you purchase line from the tackle shop, avoid selecting spools that appear to have been out on display for a long time. It is always better to ask for a fresh supply that has been kept in store.

Heat is another agent that helps to weaken monofilament and one over which the angler has little control. But bulk spools stored at home can and should be kept away from heat.

But now, having described the shortcomings of nylon monofilament, for all its faults it is a vast improvement on the materials the angler in the past had to use: horse-hair, strands of silkwork gut, cuttyhunk, jute, threads of all kinds — anything that a hook could be tied to without snapping at the first slight pull from a fish. Today's anglers should be grateful for that man-made substance we call nylon.

Finally, remember when you clean and oil your expensive reel that even a few drops of oil can cause damage to nylon. Separate the body of the reel from spool or drum and wipe surplus oil away immediately.

LINE STRENGTH

The strength of a nylon monofilament or
braided line is measured in pounds or kilos of
breaking strain. That is an indication of the
strength of the line when it left the factory —
but as we have seen, that need not mean the
strength of line when it is used at the waterside.
A number of factors can have affected its
quality while in the shop or your tackle box.

Breaking strain at the factory is measured on
special machines. A rather crude way for the
angler at home to test the breaking strain of
his line is to tie a length of it to a spring
balance, and pull against that until the line
breaks, noting the weight registered as it does
so. But this is only a rough-and-ready guide
and as we shall see later, every knot tied into a
line weakens it.

Each time he puts his rod and reel together the
prudent angler takes the end of the line from
the reel and tests it by giving it a few stout tugs.
If it has depreciated in strength then the line
will snap easily and must immediately be
discarded — not by being thrown away as it is,

but by cutting it up into short lengths, putting it in a bag and sending it away with the domestic refuse, or better still being burnt. (41, 42)

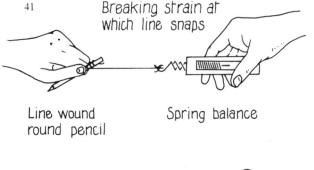

41

Breaking strain at which line snaps

Line wound round pencil

Spring balance

42

The quickest way to reduce the strength – and therefore the breaking strain — of a line is to repeatedly strain and stretch it — something that is happening all the time in angling. Line kink (constant twisting) is another strength-reducing problem and should be guarded against. Careful and thinking anglers renew all their lines at very regular intervals; they know that in the long run it is cheap.

SELECTING A LINE

The perfect line has yet to be invented. Most anglers use one line only to the exclusion of all others — even if they are unable to say why they like it. When choosing a line look for one that is pliable, though not given to over-stretching. Select one with as little glint as possible, something that if the sun catches it may put fish off from some distance, even underwater.

Many monofilament manufacturers advertise a low-glint quality with their natural-coloured lines. However, there is a great deal to be said for a coloured line either in blue, green or brown. A number of very experienced fishing enthusiasts are known to dye their lines in sections with a series of colours in an attempt to avoid glint altogether and at the same time merge it into coloured water.

BRAIDED LINES

Lines that are braided from nylon or dacron are softer than monofilament, less prone to lose strength when wet and knot easily. But they do not last long, cling when leaving the drum of a reel and also create more friction when running over the spool lip of a fixed spool reel. (43)

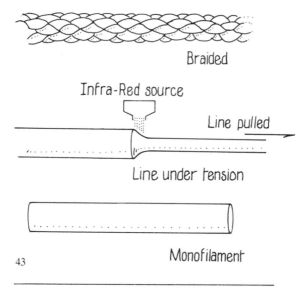

Braided

Infra-Red source

Line pulled

Line under tension

Monofilament

- Additionally, they are more easily seen by fish in the water because of their considerably thicker diameter, much thicker than monofilament. Their qualities make them excellent for sea fishing or trolling, but not for general use by the freshwater angler, who needs fine and sometimes very fine line which does not advertise its presence in clear, fresh shallow water inhabited by extremely wary fish.

LOADING LINE

Always load your line on to the reel so that it avoids imparting a twist or kink. In the case of centrepin and multiplying reels line can be run on in a straight, direct way (44) off the

44

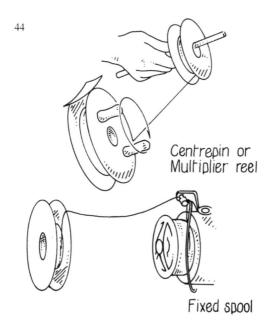

Centrepin or Multiplier reel

Fixed spool

manufacturer's spool, using a little tension to prevent the line coils bunching. Fixed-spool reels should be loaded with the line spool held at an angle of about 90 degrees, allowing the line to pull over its rim. By loading line in this fashion the bale arm will wind on without twisting the line. (44)

KNOTS

It has to be accepted that every knot that is tied in nylon monofilament will weaken the strength of the line. The amount of strength that is lost will depend on which knot has been used because some are less damaging than others. The biggest problem comes with strangulation — the knot pulls tighter and tighter until it literally cuts the line in half. The following knots have been selected because they been proved as being kind to line. They are shown in a series of step-by-step illustrations to allow you to practise tying them at home rather than at the waterside. Anyone who has tried to tie an unfamiliar knot in thin nylon, with cold, wet hands, will know what the problem is.

The Blood Knot

A universal knot where nylon line is concerned. This knot is the means whereby two ends of monofilament can be joined without their slipping apart, attaching a hook line to the reel line, or joining line to backing.

■ Start by laying both ends to be joined beside each other. (45)

45

■ Twist one free end four times round the body of the other and tuck it between the two parts. (46)

46

■ Repeat with the other end. (47)

47

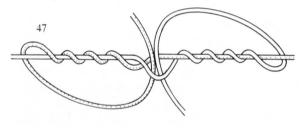

■ Draw the knot tight, remembering to moisten it before giving the final pull. This will allow it to slide easily into place without strangling. (48)

48

Tucked Half Blood Knot

This knot is used where a swivel or eyed hook needs to be attached to the line.

- Pass the end of the line through the eye. (49)

49

- Twist the end round the standing part four or five times. (50)

50

- Pass the end through the main loop (51) and —

51

- Once again through the larger loop before moistening, and pulling tight. (52)

52

Blood Loop Dropper Knot

Here is a knot for making a paternoster loop or a dropper in a fly cast.

- Make a circle with long overlapping ends and keep twisting the end around the original circle, making some 10 smaller ones. (53)

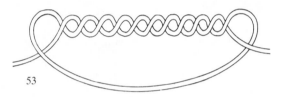

- Enlarge the centre loop and push the original circle back through it. (54)

- Moisten, then pull the ends tight holding a finger in the loop to prevent it sliding closed. (55)

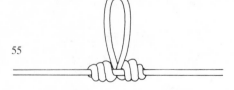

Double Loop Knot

Any time a loop is needed in the end of a line, use the double loop non-slip knot.

■ Form a bend in the end of the line. (56)

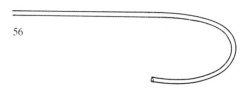

■ Make an overhand knot from it. (57)

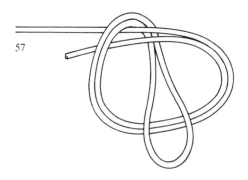

- Then make two or three more turns (58) before —

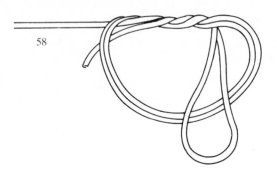

- moistening and pulling the knot tight. (59)

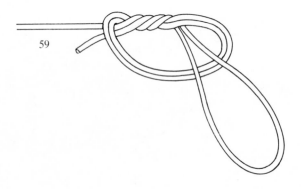

Blood Bight

Another simple knot that will form a loop quickly — even in the dark.

■ Form a loop in the end of the line. (60)

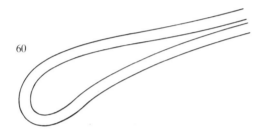

60

■ Wrap the end of the loop several times around the body. (61)

61

■ Pass the loop end back through its last turn. (62)

62

■ Moisten, then pull tight. (63)

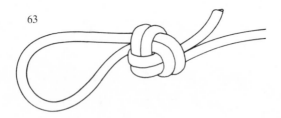

63

Dipped Loops

An easy and quick method of putting tackle together, especially hooks ready tied to nylon.

- Tie two double loop knots (see Pic. 56-59) in the end of the line, leaving the loops long.

- Pass one loop through the other and —

- Pass the hook end through the line loop

- Pull gently together. (64)

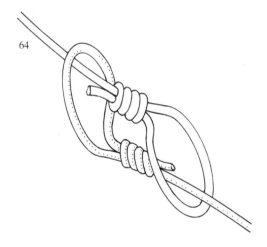

Water Knot

With a high breaking strain, the knot is useful for tying a leader with several droppers.

- Hold the ends so that there is enough overlap. (65)

65

- Form a loop and pull the right-hand end through the loop from behind making an overhand knot. (66)

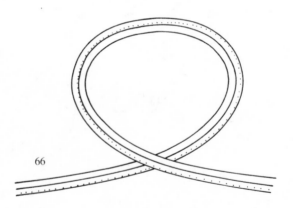

66

■ Repeat four times (67) and then —

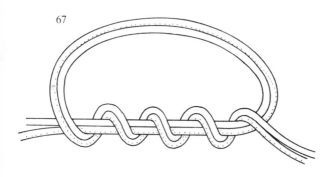

67

■ Moisten before pulling tight. The fly should be fastened to the end of line which runs towards the rod, on which the fly will stand out. (68)

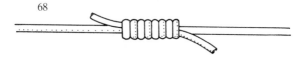

68

Spade End Knot

Often called the whipping knot, this is the universal knot for attaching spade end hooks to the hook line.

■ Lay a loop along the shank of the hook, holding both. (69)

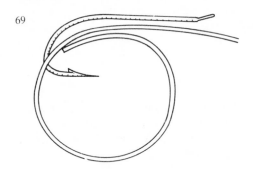

■ Make a turn round the shank over the end of the hook. (70)

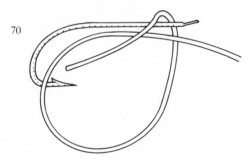

- Make another turn passing over the first. (71)

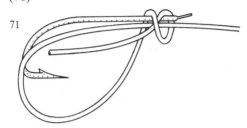

- Take five turns more along the shank. (72)

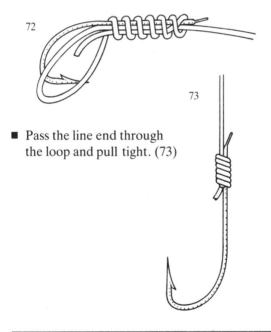

- Pass the line end through the loop and pull tight. (73)

Two-Circle Turle Knot

This is a quickly tied knot for attaching an eyed hook to the line.

- Thread the hook by its eye and make two circles, overlaying each other. (74)

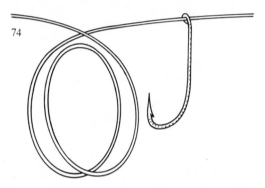

- Make an overhand knot over the loops. (75)

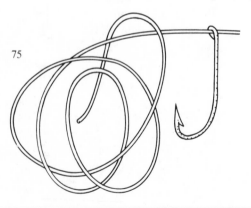

- Tighten and ease the hook through the circles. (76)

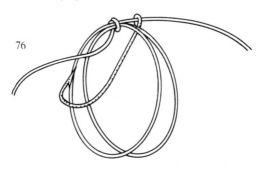

76

- Pull tight. (77)

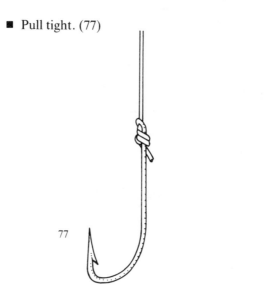

77

Domhof Knot

An exceptionally secure knot for use with eyed hooks — the line being secured around the shank of the hook as opposed to the eye. This helps make for a direct strike.

■ Pass the line through the eye and lay it along the shank to form a loop. (78)

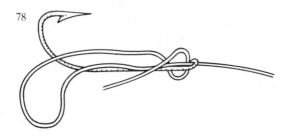

■ Take eight turns round the loop and pass the end through. (79)

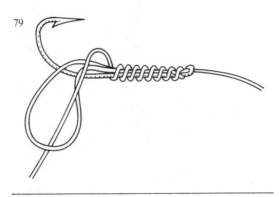

■ Moisten and pull tight. (80)

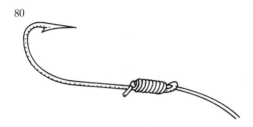

80

Buckle Swivel Loop

An easy means of attaching a buckle swivel to the line and releasing it equally quickly.

■ Make a loop in the end of the line. (81)

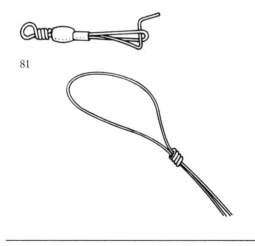

81

- Pass the loop through the eye of the swivel.
  (82)

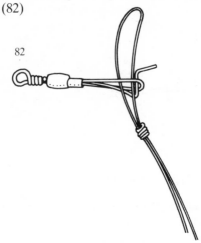

- Put the loop over the wire end of the swivel.
  (83)

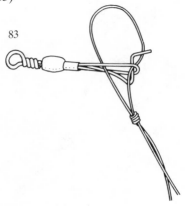

- Clear it. (84)

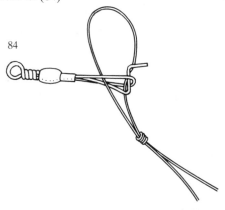

- And let it ease into place. (85)

Barrel, or Stop Knot

An adjustable knot for use with a sliding float.
The knot will wind onto the line easily.

- ■ Take 6 in of line similar to that being used
  and loop it along the line where the stop is
  required. (86)

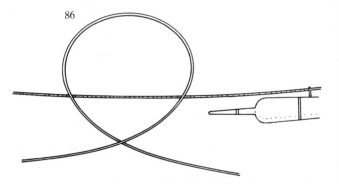

- ■ Pass one end over the reel line five or six
  times. (87)

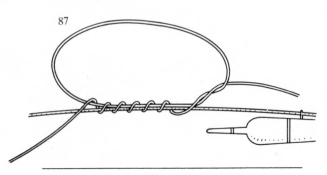

- Hold the reel line firm and pull both ends of the loop to form a solid knot. (88)

- Cut the ends free. (89)

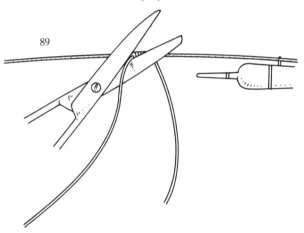

- The finished knot. (90)

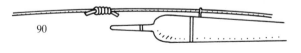

The knots described above will take an angler through his fishing career. There is one salient test for a knot in nylon: its tying must not affect the line's breaking strain, for a badly tied knot will exert sufficient pressure on itself to snap the weakest part. There are many knots of great assistance to those anglers who carry out their fishing from boats. The half-hitch, clove hitch, bowline, reef, sheet bend, all have their value when afloat. One novel sea angler's knot is the Policanski, which forms a strong attachment to a swivel. But knot tying is an exact art, perhaps a science. Anglers interested should read the knot sections in encyclopedias, for they may well discover a use for a knot so far unrecognised as having an application in the sport.

SWIVELS, LINKS AND WEIGHTS

SWIVELS AND LINKS: INTRODUCTION

For those anglers who spin or who use live or deadbaits for pike and perch fishing, the swivel is an essential piece of angling equipment. It is almost impossible to eliminate line kink altogether, because every time a hard-fighting fish is played some twist and kink is caused to the line, but swivels can reduce the nuisance drastically, something that will keep the breaking strain of the line high and prolong its life.

Swivels and links are small items of tackle that cost mere pence, but they are probably the most abused and misunderstood aids in the myriad of angling's fishing accessories. For many anglers their presence is regarded as essential and any old swivel — the first that comes to hand — is fitted somewhere along the line. In fact there are a number of different swivels and links on the market and using the wrong one can be more counter-productive than using none at all.

In exactly the same way as hooks, swivels are sized and numbered, the smallest being size

18, the largest 8/0, designed for heavy sea fishing, are immensely strong. Like hooks, the more you pay then the higher the quality and, more important still, the better they will revolve. Good swivels are bronzed — the best are manufactured from stainless steel. Some have ball-bearings incorporated in the housing and there are a number of brass swivels on the market but these are intended for sea fishing and tend to wear quite quickly.

Box Swivels

■ Box swivels are among the earliest form of swivel and they are still manufactured and readily available from tackle shops. Though they were designed for sea fishing they are available in smaller sizes suitable for coarse fishing. In terms of efficiency they are poor performers, the pull through the swivel jamming the moving parts against the body of the swivel itself. Box swivels are also capable of picking up grit and weed in the exposed moving parts — although, on the plus side, this can be seen and removed. They are better left alone by the freshwater angler because for his special purposes there are better kinds. (91)

91

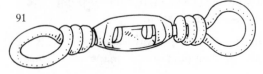

Barrel Swivels

■ These are by far the most common swivel
for freshwater fishing. They are available in
blued steel and are long lasting.
Unfortunately, by virtue of their
construction, they allow grit and dirt to
enter into the concealed body and after a
little use fail to turn at all. They should be
constantly checked while in use. (92)

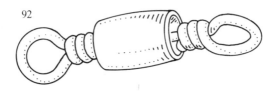

92

Ball Bearing Swivels

■ The best of all swivels — but because they
are the best they are the most expensive. A
high quality metal body incorporates ball
bearings that ensure the swivel will not jam
regardless of the pressure and pull that is
applied to it. (93)

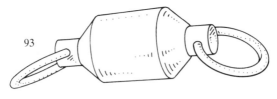

93

Three-Way Swivels

- These are designed for use with the paternoster rig, where special three-way swivels eliminate a great deal of line twist not just to the reel line, but to the trace as well. The smaller sizes are expensive but well worth the initial outlay. (94)

94

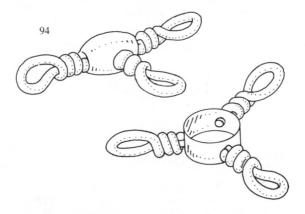

LINK SWIVELS

Link swivels are designed to allow quick attachment and release of the line, at the same time helping eliminate line kink. There are several models on the market with different methods of attachment and it is worth remembering that the simplest is the best. This especially applies when the angler is fishing on a bitterly cold day, and is trying to change a lure or hook link with frozen fingers.

Link Swivel

- The link is operated by being compressed between finger and thumb, allowing the loop of a hook link or lure to be slid into the swivel centre. These swivels are useful in large sizes — but unless the metal is of good quality, link swivels are likely to pull straight in the smaller ranges. (95)

95

Spring Link Swivel

■ One of the most commonly used of all
swivels. The sprung half circles at the link
end are prised open and line or lure passed
between and into the link's centre. These
are not the best of swivels — there is a
tendency for the half circles to open during
use, loosening the attachment that is being
used. They are also difficult to manipulate
during cold weather when fingers are wet
and clumsy. (96)

2 kinds of
Spring Link swivel

96

Buckle Link Swivel

■ Principally an item from the sea angler's
tackle box, the buckle link is simple to use
and rarely becomes prised open. It is
unfortunate that buckle link swivels are

only available in large sizes, so the
freshwater angler misses out. (97)

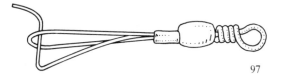

97

Snap Link Swivels

- Universally used and provided they are
  manufactured from good-quality metal, and
  with the clip end well-tempered, snap link
  swivels are highly efficient. When using
  snap link swivels, watch that a build up of
  trapped weed at the snap end doesn't gag
  the locking pieces open. (98)

Snap Link swivel

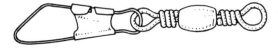

Snap Link Diamond Eye

98

CARE OF SWIVELS

During the course of just a few days fishing all swivels can become jammed with grit and dried weed which forces its way into the body and stops that all-important anti-kink action. This happens to a lesser degree with the ball bearing swivel too, but even these require some servicing if they are to give of their best.

- Before the fishing season opens, check all swivels at home and look for signs of wear at the loop end — friction from nylon line can cut into soft metal with ease.

- Drop these swivels into an egg cup and add some Swarfega or other recommended degreasant to help clean out trapped dirt.

- Wash the swivels well in water, and dry them thoroughly — a little heat will help evaporate moisture.

- Oil with a little WD 40 or similar light oil.

ANTI-KINK DEVICES

These are designed to help the anti-kink action of swivels, the best kinds attaching to the body of the swivel itself to prevent it from revolving.

K'neverkink

- The simplest anti-kink device, now well established and a great favourite, this torpedo-shaped plastic tube slips onto the line and is then pushed down onto the swivel itself. Not 100 per cent efficient, but is easy to mount and cheap enough to lose without too much financial embarrassment. (99)

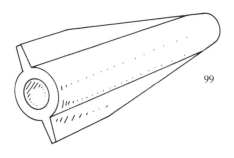

99

Plastic Vane and Swivel

■ This is another simple device. Hanging
down from the body of the swivel, the vane
prevents the body twisting and makes it
work efficiently. It is not cheap, and is
prone to snapping free when a lure is
retrieved through heavy weed. Problems
can be overcome by giving them occasional
checks. (100)

Clear plastic vane
with ball bearing swivel

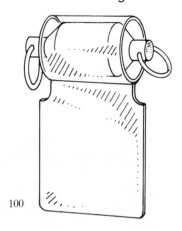

100

Swivel with Celluloid Vane

- Here is probably the most certain method of preventing line kink. The vane end is tied to the reel link, the swivel receiving the hook link or trace. If there is any disadvantage in this device it is that fish will occasionally be tempted to strike at the vane and not at the hook-bearing lure behind it. (101)

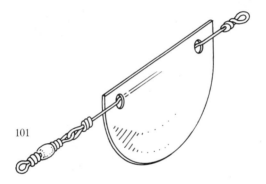

101

WEIGHTS

The use of lead weights to prevent line turning is the principle of the half-moon lead which clips onto the reel line above the swivels. A similar action is provided with the aid of the Hillman spinning lead which clips into one eye of the swivel, using its weight to stop it from turning and thereby improving its efficiency.

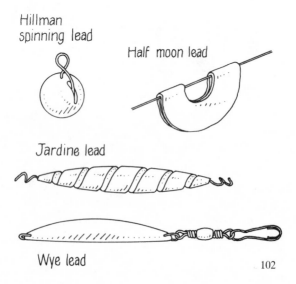

Hillman
spinning lead

Half moon lead

Jardine lead

Wye lead

102

The Wye lead with a link swivel is slightly boat-shaped and this stops the line from turning, causing the swivel to revolve. (102)

All of these devices possess a serious disadvantage in that they will make the bait 'keyhole'. Being heavy, there is a tendency for the weight to lead the bait when the cast is made, causing the two elements of the tackle to tangle together during flight. This can be avoided by reducing the weight of lead used — but the result is usually a reduction in the efficiency of the anti-kinking action. (103)

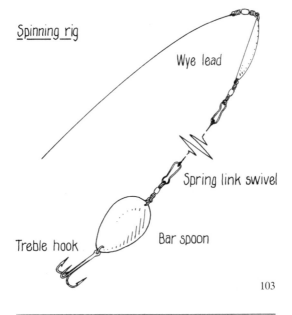

<u>Spinning rig</u>

Wye lead

Spring link swivel

Treble hook

Bar spoon

103

INDEX